A CASE FOR
Character

Also by THE Life@Work Co.™

A Case for Calling
A Case for Skill
A Case for Serving

THE Life@Work Co.™

A CASE FOR
Character

Discovering the Difference a Godly Man Makes in His Life at Work

DR. STEPHEN GRAVES & DR. THOMAS ADDINGTON

Cornerstone *Alliance*
FAYETTEVILLE, ARKANSAS 72702

Published by Cornerstone Alliance
Post Office Box 1928
Fayetteville, AR 72702

ISBN 1-890581-02-X

Cover design by Sean Womack of Cornerstone Alliance.

Printed in the United States of America

1 3 5 7 9 10 8 6 4 2

To our children

Katelyn, Julianne, Kile
Kim, Sally, Joel

Remember Proverbs 22:1.

Series Introduction

O ur offices are on the fourth floor of the second tallest building in northwest Arkansas. We have an extraordinary view of the rolling hills of Fayetteville from our panoramic picture windows. Although our city is growing, it still has the feel of a small town. Almost everyone knows almost everyone.

From that vantage point we enjoy watching cycles of life unfold around us. Unlike some parts of the country, we benefit from the whole assortment of seasons. The snowy mantle of winter melts into the sweaty heat of summer, with all variations in between.

We also watch the daily routine of hundreds of businesses. At the start of a day we can see the lights of other businesses coming on, like eyes popping open after a good night's sleep. At the end of a day we witness those same lights going out. The next morning it begins all over again. Then again. Then again.

We talk to many men for whom that description sums up their work experience. People come and go; accounts open and close. Creditors get paid; customers get billed. We pick up; we deliver. We punch in; we punch out. The workday begins, then ends. We earn our money; we spend our money. The cycle is unrelenting and unending. Then the cycle quits, and we die.

Is that all there is? Is routine drudgery what a man should expect from his work life and career?

What is the difference in the behavior and experience of a Christian man in his work compared to that of a non-Christian man?

What does it mean to be a Christian who practices dentistry? Does it mean that I have Bible verses on my business card? Do I share Christ with patients while they are under anesthesia? Or perhaps I ought to treat only Christian patients. If someone doesn't pay me, should I send their bill into collections, or should I forgive the debt and maybe pay for it myself? Should I work longer hours to display an incredible work ethic? Or maybe I need to work shorter hours so that I can spend more time with my family or serve on a church or community committee. Do I pay my employees more than the national average? Or do I pay them less so they can learn to live by faith?

What does it mean to be a Christian plumber? Do I cut my rates for Christian customers? Should I work on Sunday, or do I fail to respond to a crisis that comes on the Sabbath? Perhaps I need to hand out gospel tracts to other subcontractors on the job. Should I release one of my crew if he's incompetent? Or are Christians bound to keep every employee on the payroll for life? What does the Bible say about work?

A number of years ago we came across a verse in the New Testament book of Acts that serves as God's final epitaph for King David:

> When David had served God's purpose in his own generation, he fell asleep. (Acts 13:36)

Those words complete a description of David found way back in the Old Testament book of Psalms:

> He chose David his servant and took him from the sheep pens; from tending the sheep he brought him to be the shepherd of his people Jacob, of Israel his inheritance. And David shepherded them with integrity of heart; with skillful hands he led them. (Psalm 78:70-72)

David was a shepherd, a musician, a soldier, and a king. He had a very busy, full, and successful career. We would like to use those verses about David as the basis for exploring the making of a godly man in and through his work world. This short series will consist of four parts:

....David... *served God's purpose...*:   A Case for Calling
He chose *David his servant...*:   A Case for Serving
....David shepherded them
      with *integrity of heart*:   A Case for Character
....with *skillful hands* he led them: A Case for Skill

So, we are back to one of our questions from above. Is work basically an unending and unfulfilling cycle of activity? Answer: it depends. On what? On whether or not I know God.

According to King Solomon, one of the wisest and wealthiest men of all time:

A man can do nothing better than to eat and drink and find satisfaction in his work. This too, I see, is from the hand of God.... *To the man who pleases him, God gives wisdom, knowledge and happiness, but to the sinner he gives the task of gathering and storing up wealth to hand it over to the one who pleases God.* (Ecclesiastes 2:24-26; italics added)

Without God in my life, I might be driven, full of ambition, and very successful. I might even make it to the pinnacle of my profession. But I will not enjoy my work over time. It will not bring me fulfillment. I will be on a treadmill.

These books address a Christian man in the workplace. The definition and clarity that the Bible brings to a man and his work world are reserved for those who enjoy a personal relationship with Jesus. If you don't know Him, we strongly urge you to invite Him into your life. Then join us in exploring the topic of work in the incredibly rich, amazingly untapped pages of Scripture.

> May the favor of the Lord our God rest upon us;
> establish the work of our hands for us—
> yes, establish the work of our hands. (Psalm 90:17)

A word about our writing style. As coauthors, we speak in the first person when telling a story that relates to one of us as individuals. But we do not identify who belongs to which story. To help unravel that mystery, the following are some personal characteristics that will help sort us out.

Steve is an avid fisherman who baited hooks as a young boy on the Mississippi Gulf Coast. His appetite for learning and his energy for making friends have trademarked his twenty-three years of ministry and business.

Tom grew up in Hong Kong as the son of a medical missionary. He spent a number of years driving eighteen-wheelers, and he has taught at three universities.

We live in Fayetteville, Arkansas, love Scripture, and work together as business partners. Our companies and colleagues do work in organizational consulting and publishing. We have a passion to understand biblical principles that apply to work.

Book Introduction

Character matters.

Personality helps. Drive and focus make a difference. Passion plays a part. Training and education certainly make their contribution. But don't go to work without character. As a matter of fact, don't hire someone who doesn't have proven character. Don't partner with another business, either downstream or upstream, that doesn't have people of character. Don't build your best friendships with people who are bankrupt of sound, sturdy, good character. Why?

Because character matters.

This book will help establish what character is, reveal where character is developed, and then portray a series of snapshots of character on display.

Definition of Character

The sum of my behaviors,
public and private,
consistently arranged
across the spectrum
of my life.

"He chose David...to be the shepherd of his people Jacob.... And David shepherded them with integrity of heart" (Psalm 78:70-72).

CONTENTS

CHAPTER ONE

What Character Looks Like

Most of the world thought they had lost a treasured businessman of international repute when Armand Hammer died in December of 1990. He had built Occidental Petroleum into a worldwide powerhouse, and as chairman of the board, he consummated deals while globe-trotting in his private Boeing 727 jet.

He was known as a personal adviser to almost all United States presidents from Franklin D. Roosevelt to George Bush. His Rolodex listed virtually every government head in every country of significance, including the Communist nations that were out-of-bounds to United States citizens during the Cold War era. He enjoyed the company of Prince Charles of Great Britain. He cut exclusive business deals with Lenin, Brezhnev, Gorbachev, and other leaders of the Soviet Union. He purchased an interest in Arm & Hammer Baking Soda because its name coincided with his own. He won lucrative oil contracts in Qaddafi's Libya. His airplane crisscrossed the globe constantly, touching down in countries like Iran and Iraq, Nigeria, and China. He collected some of the best art in the world. He sponsored conferences on peace and human rights. Armand Hammer may literally have known more world leaders across a wider spectrum of countries and over a greater span of years than any other human being of his era.

It seems that Armand Hammer's life turned out to be ninety-two years of a carefully crafted charade. From the earliest years of his association with the Soviet Union, he funneled money into a vast Soviet spy network in the United States. Many of his companies were primarily fronts that allowed him to launder money for the Soviet regime. Hoover's FBI investigated him. He bought politicians around the world. Bribes and illegal secret deals brought him many of his business contracts.

Hammer used and discarded wives and numerous other women. In one case he arranged for his mistress of the moment to have plastic surgery and change her name so that his wife would not suspect an affair. His father went to jail twice for crimes that Armand had committed. He built one entire business on selling fake art that unsuspecting customers all over the United States thought were genuine articles from the Faberge and Romanoff treasures in Russia. He fathered children whom he would not acknowledge and whom he tried to hide. His last wife accused him of defrauding her of her wealth, and after she died, her estate sued him for $440 million. His own son refused to attend his father's funeral.

Armand Hammer's life was a torrid and tangled mess of promises not kept, obligations not met, and corruption left unchecked. His major problem—he had bad character.[1]

It's engraved in everyone.

Everyone has character, and it can be described: Bad. Good. Weak. Sturdy. Dark. Sterling. Psalm 78:72 sums up David's character as "integrity of heart." The Old Testament concept of integrity is one of "wholeness" and "blamelessness." A person of integrity, according to the Old Testament understanding, is a "what you see on the outside is what you get on the inside" individual. A man of authenticity and transparency. Someone who lives out in action what he believes in his head. A man of integrity is a "whole" person, the opposite of a two-faced hypocrite.

David, in the Old Testament, is a good example of setting and raising the character standard. Despite some serious sins with Bathsheba and her husband, Uriah, for example, the way he dealt with his relationship to God and people—even the way he dealt with his own sins—gives us a picture of, as the Scriptures describe him, a man after God's own heart.

Character comes from the Greek word describing a marking and engraving instrument. The picture is of an artist who wears a groove on a metal plate by repeatedly etching in the same place with a sharp tool. My character is forged as a set of distinctive marks that, when taken together, draw a portrait of who I really am.

It's based on behavior.

Behavior and character are linked together, but they are not the same thing. Behavior is what I do, one action at a time. "I behaved badly in that situation." Character is the sum of all my behavior, both public and private, arranged as patterns across the entire spectrum of my life. Any behavior, duplicated and reduplicated, forms a part of my character.

Repeated patterns of behavior wear a series of grooves, which, when put all together, form a portrait of me as a person or show a picture of my character. Sometimes that portrait is compelling and attractive; sometimes it is ugly and repelling. Usually it is a combination of the two. Even great faces have wrinkles and warts.

Governing my character is very different from knowing my gift mix and internal wiring (see *A Case for Calling*, Addington and Graves). Those were built into me by God when He created me. I am gifted and wired to be able to do certain things incredibly well; I have a bent towards some activities and against others; I am attracted to certain tasks and repelled by others. No matter how hard I work at improving my ability in certain areas, I may never be able to do them as well as someone else who is gifted and wired for those situations.

However, I have control over my character. I can improve it, change it, modify it, and compromise it. In a world where we seem to have little control, we call the shots when it comes to whether or not our character is diminished. Job said to his friends concerning his character: "I will not deny my integrity. I will maintain my righteousness and never let go of it; my conscience will not reproach me as long as I live" (Job 27:5-6). If my character goes down, I am the only one who can be blamed. No other person apart from me can allow my character to be compromised.

It's built over time.

Character comes in bits and pieces, not as a complete package. David's character was forged over many years and at least four careers. It came with time, and it came in parts, not all at once. Early in his career he was very quick to take offense and revenge. When Nabal refused to feed David and his men in 1 Samuel 25, David's hair-trigger response to the four hundred soldiers under his command was: "Put on your swords!" Nabal would have died an ugly death had his wife, Abigail, not personally intervened and begged David to leave her husband alone.

Contrast that event with one much later in David's kingship. During a very difficult time in David's reign over Israel, when his own son had conspired to steal the throne, a man named Shimei cursed David as the king fled from his palace and the city of Jerusalem. Second Samuel 16 gives a record of the incident:

> As he cursed, Shimei said, "Get out, get out, you man of blood, you scoundrel! The Lord has repaid you for all the blood you shed in the household of Saul, in whose place you have reigned. The Lord has handed the kingdom over to your son Absalom. You have come to ruin because you are a man of blood!" Then Abishai son of Zeruiah said to the king, "Why should this dead dog curse my lord the king? Let me go over

and cut off his head." But the king said, "What do you and I have in common, you sons of Zeruiah? If he is cursing because the Lord said to him, 'Curse David,' who can ask, 'Why do you do this?'" David then said to Abishai and all his officials, "My son, who is of my own flesh, is trying to take my life. How much more, then, this Benjamite! Leave him alone; let him curse, for the Lord has told him to. It may be that the Lord will see my distress and repay me with good for the cursing I am receiving today." So David and his men continued along the road while Shimei was going along the hillside opposite him, cursing as he went and throwing stones at him and showering him with dirt. (2 Samuel 16:7-13)

Building character is a day-by-day, lifetime commitment. As we allow the Holy Spirit to work in our lives and chip away at our character one piece at a time, we will be different men over time. Our character will improve. David's character did not look the same before as it did after.

It's tested over time.

We have been in business together for seven years. At the very beginning of our association, we laid out common core values to help define our relationship with each other as well as define the behavior of our organization. Those values include statements such as "We will improve each other" and "We will finish well."

We are very different men today than we were seven years ago. Our characters have been tested. They have improved. In the context of our work world, we have confronted, and in some cases continue to confront, issues such as controlling anger, keeping promises, treating colleagues as valued assets, and telling the truth. We deal with our egos and defensiveness, our ambition and stress.

Our work world is a laboratory for the improvement of our character. Every work situation is. It is often not easy. But it is always valuable.

Every single day of our work lives we take hundreds of actions. We make behavior choices scores of times. When we sum up all of those individual behaviors over an hour, then a day, then a week, then a month, then a decade, we have patterns of behavior. Those patterns of behavior make up our character.

CHAPTER TWO

How Character Is Built

I was busy working my "to do" list. It was a Monday afternoon, and my secretary said my wife was on the line. In our office we have an agreement that family calls are always pushed through—regardless. That brief phone call on that Monday afternoon shook me to the very center of my life. One of my good friends had suddenly been diagnosed with multiple myeloma, a serious form of cancer. He is my age and has four boys all still at home. He and his wife are both physicians. He is a man after God's heart. We go to church together, and our kids attend school together. Just last Friday night we had huddled together in warm blankets to watch a cold Arkansas high school football game.

Since that day, I have spent a lot of time with him. God had clearly called me to come alongside him. I thought it was so I could be of help to him during this perilous journey. However, after my first encounter, I realized that I was the beneficiary of the relationship, not my friend. God wanted to teach me something, not him. He and his family were helping me. They were helping me understand that a man's character is built day by day, decision by decision, over the years.

We cannot grow character through a crash-course weekend seminar when one day we suddenly realize we need some. It's impossible. We can't become an astronaut, or a world-class fly fisherman, or an expert brick mason in a microwave weekend of learning.

This encounter caused me to ask the question, "From where does this kind of character come?" I began to reflect deeper than I had in a long time on the issue of a man and his character. When and how had this friend of mine, his wife, and even his children developed such strong, sturdy, personal, and family character? From where does good character come?

Good character is built on a good heart.

Jesus, as He was developing a team of leaders, taught it this way, "No good tree bears bad fruit, nor does a bad tree bear good fruit. The good man brings good things out of the good stored up in his heart, and the evil man brings evil things out of the evil stored up in his heart" (Luke 6:43, 45).

A friend of mine used to say that when a man gets squeezed, whatever is in him will come out. Work has a way of squeezing a man. From those pressure points come our reflexes and reactions. It is our reflexes and reactions that publicize what is in our heart.

In the last couple of years I've observed a number of men who received the dreadful communication that their job would be changing, and sometimes the change was to be dramatic. For instance, one of my friends found out the week before Christmas that the following Friday would be his last day with his company. This man had been with his company a long time. He had poured his talents into the company, and the company had rewarded him well in the past. But suddenly those at the top felt it would be financially and strategically shrewd to "lose a couple of layers and dissolve two departments." Robert's job was gone.

He called me, and we met for a quick lunch as he replayed the story. I remember saying to him, "So, Robert, what are you going to do?"

He looked back with a little hesitation and said, "I'm going to take about a week and do some 'heart work.'"

To that, I asked, "What do you mean?"

He said, "I want to make sure I learn what I need to learn in this situation. I want to make sure that this situation makes me a better man, not a bitter man. I don't want to rationalize away some of the feedback points, nor do I want to build a wall of resentment and revenge toward my company and my boss. And, most of all, I want to make sure that I guard myself from a quick reflex of 'I've got to go out and fix my problem.' I want to make sure that I am genuinely trusting the Lord as I clean up my resume—which I haven't done in almost twenty years—and start knocking on doors."

That's character. That's a good heart.

Integrity doesn't just happen. It is planted like a seed in a man's heart where it is watered and nourished, and day by day, year by year, it develops. Some men are "built to last." Others are not. The difference is clearly the character factor.

Our culture is enamored with leadership. It should be enamored with character. Every legitimate survey done by pollsters in the last few years consistently shows that integrity, honesty, and credibility are common characteristics of superior leaders.[1] We cannot acquire these qualities simply by reading a book on "being a leader" or listening to another speech on "successful leaders." Leaders have character that has grown from the soil of a good heart, and what is in us comes out when we do "life at work."

Therefore it is critical that a man build and protect a strong, pure heart. The heart is the seat of the inner man. It comprises such elements as feelings, desires, affections, motives, will, intellect, and principles. It is in the heart that

- We process life.
- We ponder eternity.
- We transmit heritage to our children.
- We engage in real worship.
- We filter negative emotions.
- We conquer sin cycles.
- We initiate decision making.
- We forge good character.
- We knit real friendships.
- We confirm personal significance.
- We communicate to God.

As a man's heart goes, so goes the man.

Sound character sits on a solid sense of truth.

When Paul the Apostle saw the vision of Jesus on the Damascus road, he didn't change jobs; he simply changed hearts. Instead of building pagans and fighting Christians, he switched to building Christians and fighting pagans. When Paul was on assignment in Thessalonica with a handful of believers, an interesting reference to character emerges as Paul evaluated those with whom he had come in contact: "Now the Bereans were of more noble character than the Thessalonians, for they received the message with great eagerness and examined the Scriptures every day to see if what Paul said was true" (Acts 17:11).

Sound character has to be wrapped around more than an optimistic, self-willed "I will not lie," "I will not steal," or "I will not get even." We must have truth at the core, or our convictions will unravel in times of challenge. Truth acts as an internal foundation that keeps character grounded. There must be some substance, not just style. Companies and organizations struggle with this every day.

Over the last few years, our company has helped many companies generate something called a core-values statement. Our own company's core-values statement can serve as an example.

CORNERSTONE COMPANIES CORE VALUES

How We Think:

We are overt regarding our Christian commitment and agenda.

We cultivate core competencies in both Bible and business.

We adjust our agenda to fit God's personal and super-natural direction.

How We Work:

We under-promise and over-deliver.
We plan the work and work the plan.
We coordinate our work with all who are involved.
We upgrade our individual and collective capabilities.
We do the right thing regardless of the consequence.
We accept clients based on the potential to effect
meaningful and lasting change.

How We Behave:

We build healthy relationships.
We improve each other.
We focus on and abandon ourselves to the strengths
of others.
We work hard, play hard, and share the reward.
We finish well.

A core-values statement certainly is not the only critical document that helps any organization become a world-class enterprise. But it is the core-values system that prescribes behavior for its personnel. However, we have learned that core values must belong to the individual people themselves. Values cannot be passed down as Moses did the tablets. It takes more than framing them in a plaque or putting them into a wallet card to make them operational. It takes each employee, one at a time, saying, "What do these values mean to me at my work-station?"

A boss can mandate performance, but he cannot mandate character. We trust, hope, and pray that people do the right thing when we are not there and maybe when no one at all is there. That is why some people say character is what we are in the dark. But they will not do the right thing unless they know what is right and have settled the difference in their souls.

PERSONAL CONVICTIONS

The highway for character to be expressed in a man's life begins with his having sound, solid, personal convictions. What is a conviction? "A conviction is a category of God's thinking on a particular that I wholeheartedly embrace and act upon with determination." Perhaps no biblical example has more to say about character in the workplace than Daniel. With him, we watch character in the making, and we watch character on display. From his life we learn many lessons on character and convictions.

1. *Sometimes the biggest test of our convictions comes when we are detached from our comfortable Christian subculture.* Daniel had been uprooted, transplanted, given a new name, and jerked from his environment. All external anchors had been stripped. He alone was grounded in his own convictions and character (Daniel 1:1-4).

2. *Our world will aggressively attack and challenge our Christian convictions.* Young Daniel was offered food he was not supposed to eat. He was given a new education and even had his name changed. His environment had done everything possible to soften his firm stand on right and wrong. But he didn't break. As a matter of fact, he didn't even bend (Daniel 1:5-8).

3. *The display of firm Christian convictions does not have to be obnoxious and disgusting.* Daniel didn't say, "I'm a Jew, you idiot; I can't eat your food." Instead, he balanced his convictions with his desire to have positive influence and impact. This is a difficult truth for many

Christians to accept. Not Daniel. This quality could have been the quality that enabled him to serve four different administrations (Daniel 1:9-14).

4. *Holding to clear biblical convictions always carries consequences.* A display of character starts with a man knowing in his mind what is right and wrong. It is deep-seated, personalized truth that is at the base of sound, consistent decision making, which is the steel frame for sturdy character.

One of my partners met a gentleman at a strategic planning summit our company was leading for one of our clients. My partner commented, "This is a great guy. We need to spend more time with him." I've learned that some people get worse the more we get to know them, and others just unfold depth upon depth. The more we peel back, the more we find that impresses us. This man was clearly on the deep end of the pool in his character. So, a few months later we had the occasion of spending the morning with him on the East Coast. Through the conversation that morning, we learned that the man had been financially very successful years ago. But "when the market turned," he had lost everything and ended up owing creditors more than $60 million. His testimony was that although he had struggled, he knew he had to pay back every dollar. So he constructed a pay-back plan, contacted everyone, and pledged his word to clear his debt.

Last year he made his last payment for a $20,000 debt to a small bank in the Southeast. He personally drove to the bank and handed the check to the banker, who said, "I thought you would never do this."

This modern-day Daniel said, "I didn't have a choice, it was the right thing to do. I knew it years ago, and it has never left me." Opinions are something we hold, whereas convictions are something that hold us.

Good character keeps good company.

We all know this to be true when we are young and little; we just forget that it's still true as we get older. I can remember my mom instructing me to stay away from Jimmy down the street. "He's a rotten apple," she would say. (Of course we wonder how many moms were saying that about us back then.) We all know what that means. It means the same thing that Paul meant when he said decisively, "Bad company corrupts good character" (1 Corinthians 15:33). But who cautions us of rotten apples when life graduates us to our twenties, thirties, forties, and beyond?

I sat down the other day and analyzed all the relationships in my world. I broke them down into four apple categories in honor of my mother. There were healthy apples, bruised apples, rotten apples, and poisonous apples.

The healthy apples were, of course, those people who are nutritious and refreshing. Contact with them leaves us robust, hearty, and healthy. And we hope it works both ways.

Then there are the bruised apples. A bite will not make us sick, but it doesn't contribute to our health either.

Third, there are the rotten apples. Those are the people in our lives who truly have a negative impact upon us. By constantly digesting their influence, we will get sick. It is a fact.

Finally, there are poisonous apples, for which some people have a steady appetite. They are captured in a web of friendship that is killing them. Usually those captured have a hard time seeing the destructive friendship. Others around usually see a lot more clearly than we do at this point.

Walter (not his real name) was self-employed. Even as a youngster, his entrepreneurial bent was noticed. His latest career was the launching of his own communication and advertisement company. He had landed a big first account that hurled him forward. Starting strong was never Walter's problem.

It was sometime after year four that his wife first probed and asked Walter why he was slowly changing and becoming someone different than the man she had married. His reflex response was that she was making it all up and they both were getting older. Then the kids started commenting, and finally a couple of his best friends began probing. As the story unraveled, the rotten apple was exposed. Walter had experienced a surge of growth in his third year of business, and as always, business growth takes capitalization. Walter couldn't self-fund the opportunities that lay ahead of them. And like any red-blooded American entrepreneur, he put together a "deal" to bring in some outside investors. The only criteria for his investor profile was "anyone who would give him lots of money." It turned out that he had partnered with a man who had none of Walter's values and none of Walter's convictions. Eventually, someone was going to affect someone, and in the long run, Walter was affected.

He began to use language that, until that time, his family had never heard. He began a slow unraveling on many of his best qualities—patience, kindness, and even honesty. It came to a confrontation when his wife and one his key employees called Walter's hand on his handling of the company's income tax. He was cheating, and next he was lying. Healthy relation-

reinforce strong character, and unhealthy relationships deteriorate our character.

Good character is shaped under suffering.

Some things come through suffering that cannot and will not come any other way.

> I walked a mile with Pleasure,
>   She chattered all the way,
> But she left me none the wiser,
>   For all she had to say.
> I walked a mile with Sorrow,
>   And ne'er a word said she;
> But, oh, the things I learned from her
>   When Sorrow walked with me!
> —"Understanding Suffering," Robert Browning

The apostle Paul put together this flowchart, which includes both suffering and character: "We also rejoice in our sufferings, because we know that suffering produces perseverance; perseverance, character; and character, hope" (Romans 5:3-4). Most of us react when suffering hits. Some people react with denial. "This can't be happening to me," they say, burying their heads in the sand. Some people react with a kind of redirection or escapism. "I'll just go fishing all weekend, or hit 'happy hour' two hours early, or lose myself in a good book." Others are pessimists from birth. Everyone knows a couple of these people. Every time you see them, they're singing a different verse of "Nobody Knows the Trouble I've Seen." And then others respond with a shallow kind of optimism. "Well, I guess I'll just have to grin and bear it."

Tough times come to all of us. Different shapes, different sizes, different weights, but they will come. The Bible acknowledges that as a fact of life on this planet. The Epistle of James says it this way: "Consider it pure joy, my brothers, whenever you face trials of many kinds, because you know that the testing of your faith develops perseverance. Perseverance must finish its work so that you may be mature and complete, not lacking anything" (James 1:2-4). How we receive and digest suffering can become one of the greatest shapers of our character.

CHAPTER THREE

Ten Character Traits for a Godly Man

1. Maintain moral purity

If you tell the truth, you don't have to remember anything. —Mark Twain

The Promise Keepers organization constantly surveys its constituents for the purpose of sharpening their emphasis to positively impact our culture. At the end of the Promise Keepers' 1996 conference season, Christian men in America responded when asked, "What one topic do you need specific help in?" The greatest response was, "Pornography or sexual purity." The struggle continues.

Two of my friends travel a lot with their work. They are seasoned veterans of the road. They are also seasoned veterans of long and faithful marriages. Those two claims many times have trouble coexisting. Most of our consultants spend six to seven nights a month on the road. We are always thinking about the potential problem, trying to protect against moral failure. Consequently, I asked my road-veteran friends to share how they have remained faithful for all these years.

"No magic formula," they said, "but we have instituted a few practical 'hedges' around our heart, our mind, and our world." Here is how one of them answered:

Hedge #1: I have a group of men back home ask the hard questions, regularly probing for fractures in my mental or emotional armor.

Hedge #2: I try to have the movie channels in the hotel rooms disconnected in the room before I ever get there.

Hedge #3: I exercise or read a book while on a road trip.

Hedge #4: I carry lots of pictures of my wife and kids and make them a part of my road conversations with clients, friends, and even strangers.

Hedge #5: I work hard to avoid being alone with female clients at night.

Hedge #6: I always share every part of my itinerary with my secretary, my wife, and my "Gestapo" accountability team.

Hedge #7: I don't give way to the smallest temptation— no innocent baby steps toward evil.

Hedge #8: I have a group of guys back home ask the hard questions, regularly probing for fractures in my mental or emotional armor. (He knew he was repeating this hedge, but he repeated it anyway. He said these hedges are the bookends.)

I asked, "Does this really work?" to which they said, "Look, if a guy wants to cheat on his wife, he will find a way to do that. It's like your income taxes. There are general structures and guidelines that help a good man to stay good, but if a good man is determined to go bad and, in this case, cheat on his taxes, he will do it. Simply because we have forms to fill out, and an April 15 deadline every year doesn't prohibit anyone from cheating."

Moral purity starts with a firm, rigid commitment to a clean heart and a clean mind. If a man works on that and then adds some practical, useful "hedges," there is a good chance he'll stay out of the ditch.

Lust is not noticing that a woman is sexually attractive. Lust is born when we turn a simple awareness into a preoccupied fantasy. When we invite sexual thoughts into our minds and nurture them, we have passed from simple awareness into lust. Martin Luther put it this way: "We cannot help it if birds fly over our head. It is another thing if we invite them to build a nest in our hair."[1]

2. Solicit honest feedback

Do not think of yourself more highly than you ought. (Romans 12:3)

Jonathan had just received a promotion. He had worked for most of his career with the same company. His boss had received a huge promotion and would be relocating to the home office in Chicago, which would position Jonathan to manage a huge piece of the business. As a matter of fact, he would have nine directors reporting to him. He decided his first piece of business would be to sit down with the people he had been working with for the last seven years and solicit feedback on how he could improve as he moved to his new assignment. In my company, we call that kind of behavior "walking toward the barking dog." Is there a better way to get honest feedback than to ask for it?

I remember a scene four years ago when my oldest daughter was about to go into the second grade. We were in Destin, Florida, vacationing with friends. My oldest daughter and I had awakened early, so we took a hand-holding walk down the silent, still beach as we watched the sun coming up on the surf. During the walk I determined to solicit some feedback. Who better to give me a scorecard on being a daddy than my seven-year-old daughter? I took a deep breath, swallowed twice, and said, "What do you think Daddy needs to do to be a better daddy?"

She looked up ... and told me!

Whether it is feedback from a boss, an employee, a co-worker, or a six-year-old daughter, honesty sometimes hurts. But without honesty we are all reduced to an existence that teeters between hypocrisy and self-deception. Tom Peters, the American management guru, emphasized this in his best-selling book *Thriving on Chaos.* He entitles section 7 "Becoming Obsessed with Listening."[2] Although Peters was primarily emphasizing a company's need to solicit and respond to honest consumer feedback, I think the principle can still be applied to the individual. Do I want to engage in a lifetime of learning and self-improvement? Honest, objective, untarnished feedback from others is one of the surest instruments for personal growth. But it takes character to solicit feedback.

Sam Walton's success has been analyzed and praised. However, analysts on the outside oftentimes formulize Wal-Mart's success differently than the 670,000 associates on the inside. Mr. Sam consistently made trips to solicit input from his national team. He constantly asked the "What's broken" question and "What can we do about it?" Those wearing the Wal-Mart badge today smile in memory of Mr. Sam's genuine solicitation of their contribution to building Wal-Mart.

Gaining feedback requires listening. It's a skill that must be developed. Many people don't listen because they would rather speak. Many people don't listen because they have trained themselves to hear only praise. Many people don't listen because they are too busy. And many people don't listen because they don't know how to.

Soliciting feedback requires a hunger for truth and growth that only exists in the heart of character.

3. Practice real forgiveness and receive real forgiveness

Everyone says forgiveness is a lovely idea until he has something to forgive. —C.S. Lewis

My friend and I were sitting next to each other in a hot, tired gym watching our daughters play basketball. Another man came up and introduced himself to me; we chatted for a while and then he walked on down to the other end of the gym to where his daughter was practicing. My friend asked, "Do you know that guy's story?"

I said, "No, but I'd love to hear it."

He then unfolded the story that the hand-shaking stranger had stolen well over $200,000 from his employer a number of years ago. He had been caught and had gone to prison. He served his time, was released, and has returned as a refurbished part of the American workforce.

I immediately personalized the experience as I reflected back on the injuries done to me when someone had stolen from our company. I was reminded of how hard it is to forgive others when they intentionally injure us. In his book *Forgive and Forget*, Lewis Smedes says:

Only hurts that are personal, unfair, and deep require forgiveness. Slight defeats and annoyances do not require forgiveness because there was no intentional betrayal, disloyalty, or brutality involved. Forgiveness is a spiritual surgery, cutting away the wrong so the person can be seen without it. Something like peeling an orange. Forgiveness is not forgetting, excusing, smoothing things over or accepting. Quieting troubled waters is not the same as rescuing drowning people.[3]

Most work environments are staged with people, not just machinery. When people are involved, there will be mistakes and there will be misunderstandings. An employee who can't forgive will develop shallow and surface relationships and eventually begin judging the motives of all of those around him.

- Did someone forget to say thanks?
- Was I passed over for a promotion?
- Did my company let me go unfairly?
- Did someone tell me they would do something and then severely under-deliver?
- Did one of my coworkers bring a terribly bad day to work with them yesterday?

- Has someone ever judged my motives to be bad
  when they really were not?
- Do I know how to say, "I'm sorry and would you
  forgive me?"
- Do I know how to say yes and really follow through
  when someone asks for forgiveness?

Forgiveness always takes a "first stepper." Someone has to initiate the action of mending a broken fence. It will not just happen. It takes character to be a forgiver and a first stepper. Without character, forgiveness migrates to become something else.

When forgiveness puts me one up, on top, in a superior place as the benefactor, the generous one, the giver of freedom and dignity, it's not forgiveness; it's an impostor. When forgiveness ends open relationships and leaves people cautious, twice shy, safely concealed, afraid to risk free, open, spontaneous living, it's not forgiveness; it is an impostor.[4]

4. Make courageous decisions

We make our decisions, and then our decisions turn around and make us. —F.W. Boreham[5]

When Nehemiah left his post as cupbearer to Artaxerxes and moved to Jerusalem to rebuild the wall, he faced significant opposition. Their enemies threatened to undo the rebuilding of the wall. Opposition runs like a thread all the way through the book of Nehemiah. As the leader, Nehemiah was forced to deal both with the opposition and with the resulting discouragement and depression among his own people. When the people rebuilding the wall were actually threatened with bodily harm, Nehemiah made a decision to arm his own people:

Therefore I stationed some of the people behind the lowest points of the wall at the exposed places, posting them by families, with their swords, spears and bows. After I looked things over, I stood up and said to the nobles, the officials and the rest of the people, "Don't be afraid of them. Remember the Lord, who is great and awesome, and fight for your brothers, your sons and your daughters, your wives and your homes." When our enemies heard that we were aware of their plot and that God had frustrated it, we all returned to the wall, each to his own work. From that day on, half of my men did the work, while the other half were

equipped with spears, shields, bows and armor....
Those who carried materials did their work with one
hand and held a weapon in the other, and each of the
builders wore his sword at his side as he worked....
Neither I nor my brothers nor my men nor the guards
with me took off our clothes; each had his weapon,
even when he went for water. (Nehemiah 4:13-23)

As a result of that decision, the wall was finished, and the
people celebrated.

Character gives a man the well to draw from to hold his
stand on a hard issue. It takes courage to make good decisions
involving hard issues over that span of a man's life. Why?
Sometimes because of the external opposition around us and
sometimes because of the doubt and fear inside us. Either
attack will prey on our decision-making skill. We can either
become paralyzed with indecision and second-guessing or we
can release decision arrows that have little chance of hitting the
intended target. The effect is a bad decision, a misguided decision, or a half-baked decision.

Finishing strong over the long haul is made possible by finishing strong at single-decision intersections. Finishing strong
hourly will lead to finishing strong daily. Finishing strong daily

will lead to finishing strong weekly. Finishing strong weekly will lead to finishing strong monthly. And finishing strong monthly will lead to finishing strong yearly, which will position a man to finish life well at his last lap.

5. Remain flexible

We cannot direct the wind, but we can adjust the sails.[6]

Scripture is full of examples of men of God who had to change their plans to fulfill God's purposes. In the book of Genesis, Joseph had to leave his home in Canaan and take up residence in Egypt. He did not want to go, but having the strength of character to remain obedient to God, he flourished in spite of the unfairness of his brothers and his Egyptian masters.

Daniel also was taken captive from Israel to Babylon, controlled by a ruthless regime. As part of God's plan, Daniel served as a high administrator under four separate rulers in two kingdoms. He ended up being highly influential, introducing kings in both the Babylonian and Medo-Persian empires to the one true God. His influence also paved the way for the return of the Jewish exiles to Jerusalem and Israel.

Nehemiah was a cupbearer, or a top aid, to King Artaxerxes. Because of the burden that God placed on Nehemiah's heart, he left a very secure, comfortable, and influential position to go to Jerusalem to rebuild the walls around that city that had been destroyed when Jerusalem was overrun and pillaged.

Joseph, Daniel, and Nehemiah were, according to Scripture, in the center of God's will in the process of moving from one context of service into another.

Most people don't like change. Change usually means pain, and, naturally, we hate to hurt. Therefore, we tend to get comfortable with business as usual. Being a change leader, change agent, and a willing follower of change is crucial to most personal and corporate success.

One of my partners and I have adopted the "four immutable laws of international travel."

1. It could turn out just like you planned.
2. It could turn out better than you planned.
3. It could turn out worse than you planned.
4. It could turn out "different" than you planned.

So also goes life. Rarely does life happen "just as we planned." It might be worse, it might be better, but it certainly is usually "different." Obviously, we would not be discounting planning. We have built a part of our business on training organizations in an integrated, strategic planning process. Planning, organization, and forethought are three expressions of God's nature that run from Genesis to Revelation. Our trouble is that once we have a plan, we curl up and get comfortable with it. And many times that produces a passive, nonengaged bystander in life.

"Many are the plans in a man's heart, but it is the Lord's purpose that prevails" (Proverbs 19:21).

6. Practice good time management

Make the best use of your time.[7]

The other day, one of our consultants said to me, "It's shocking how much wasted time or misdirected time exists in many corporations and organizations." He had just helped a company clarify roles and tasks among its management team. To do that, he had asked everyone to track their time for a couple of weeks, and then turn in the logbook. Not long after that, I heard a foreman who runs a framing crew for a local builder say, "Most workers ought to reimburse their employers 15 to

30 percent of their check every two weeks, because of their slippery, sloppy handling of time."

Time management is really a misnomer because we all have exactly the same amount of time, although some accomplish several times as much as others do with their time. Self-management is a better term because it implies that we manage ourselves and the time allotted us.[8]

The key is not simply to push harder on the pedal. To maximize the time God has given us to steward, we can't be obsessed with only revving up the rpm's. We have to become obsessed with character.

Our time is a gift, and our time is not our own! We didn't carve it out for ourselves, and rarely do we spend fifteen minutes when we are the only ones impacted if time is marginalized, misused, or squandered.

There is a delicate balance between being busy and being productive. Peter Senge in *The Fifth Discipline* establishes the case that effective workers "think and learn, not just go and do."[9] There is also a delicate balance between being available and being flexible, with being focused and being efficient. Building people is time-consuming. It always has been and always will be. Ask any effective mom or dad or ask any effective people builder. Thinking strategically is a time strangler. Reflection and evaluation can be a time burner.

Effective time management starts not on the Franklin or Day-Timer "to do" list but in the mind and heart of a man's character.

The supply of time is totally inelastic. No matter how high the demand, the supply will not go up. Time is also totally perishable and cannot be stored. Yesterday's time is gone forever and will never come back. And lastly, time is totally irreplaceable. Within limits, we can substitute one resource for another, but there is no substitute for time.[10]

7. Handle money correctly

Money is amoral, neutral, just like a handgun or morphine. Put a pistol in a hand of a policeman and it's a tool for justice. But in the hand of a criminal, it is an instrument of evil. —Pat Morely[11]

The story was almost too much for me to believe. The man had lost his wallet with all of his credit cards and important personal identification. But, as luck would have it, he had also just cashed his weekly $450 check and put all of the money in the back of his wallet.

He and his wife both worked, and every dollar was already accounted for. Each dollar had a temporary envelope at home that would regulate spending for the next seven days. The rest of the evening went terrible (as one might expect) as he and his wife lamented their loss and with anxious hearts tried to figure out what to do.

The next morning his doorbell rang. There stood two teenage boys holding his wallet, relating where they had found it. Being grateful, the man thought, "Well, maybe at least I can recover my driver's license and other identification." As he opened his wallet, to his shock, all of his credit cards were still there. And as he folded the back open, he noticed that all of his money was also still intact. Not one dollar was missing.

The man thought, "This must be an angel encounter." No pair of teenage boys in America would take the time on Saturday morning, hunt down a stranger, and return $450 in cash. The local newspaper did an interview, and even the reporter sat in disbelief as she asked the two boys, "Why did you return all of that cash?"

In response, one of the boys smiled and said, "Because it wasn't ours and it belonged to someone else."

Still struggling, the reporter continued, "Didn't you want to keep the money at all?"

These two young lads had character. It's too bad there is not a place on a resume to put this kind of life experience. For sure, I know a lot of companies that would love to have that quality of fiscal responsibility engrafted into each person on their payroll.

There are so many ditches a man can fall into regarding money! Handling money correctly can be like successfully walking from one side of a zoo to another after someone lets all of the animals out of their cages. The dangers and difficulties with money come in so many different forms of attack.

- Do I frivolously spend or unwisely invest what I make?
- Do I handle my company's money as precisely and scrupulously as I do my own?
- Do I ascribe personal value to income level?
- Are my expense reports true and accurate?
- Do I only relate to one economic slice of our society and practice discrimination against the others?
- Are my views about money too rigid, legalistic, and conservative?
- Are my views about money too loose, liberal, and slippery?

- Am I a slave to indebtedness and spending habits?
- Am I obsessed with money whether I have a lot or a little?
- Do I consider my job only as valuable as my pay-check?

It takes a man of character to handle money correctly. What should I do? View it balanced. Hold it loosely. Manage it wisely.

8. *Weather unfairness and injustice*

The same heat that melts the butter hardens the clay.[12]

A number of years ago I almost lost my life in a terrible truck accident. It was an early winter morning, and I was at the wheel of a truck, driving west on the so-called Chicago Skyway, which is an eighteen-mile toll bridge that connects the Indiana Tollway with the Chicago Loop. The roads were slippery because of the inordinate amount of snow that had fallen that winter. When a car ahead of me began to slow down, I braked, and immediately the truck went violently out of control. I slid through the median into the eastbound lane and over the edge of the bridge. My tractor-trailer fell sixty feet onto a road that ran alongside the bridge. Although it took Chicago firemen more than an hour to cut me out of my mangled vehicle, I was miraculously spared serious injury.

The company for whom I drove fired me. I ended up in the hospital, with a long recovery ahead of me, and without a job. I found out soon after the accident that the reason the truck had gone out of control was that the brakes on the steering axle had actually been disconnected by mechanics who couldn't figure out how to adjust them properly.

Injustice and unfairness are standard parts of our lives, and will be until Jesus comes again. All the way through the Old and New Testaments are examples of men who all their lives had to endure unfair treatment. None are more dramatic than the Old Testament story of a godly businessman named Job. His life opens with things going very well, only to have the bottom continuously drop out. He was served unfairness and injustice with an intensity and consistency that would make most of us do more than just ask lots of questions.

So what is supposed to be our response to unfairness and injustice?

First, don't become cynical and skeptical. Many times a series of unfair experiences will leave us riddled with a long list of negative feelings and expressions, such as "There is really no good that will ever happen or can happen to me" or "A good God doesn't exist and certainly does not have good intentions for me." Or we may begin to construe the notion that everyone in the world has a devious, dangerous agenda for us. George Maraneth, a nineteenth-century English novelist, observed, "Cynics are only happy in making the world as barren to others as they have made it for themselves."[13]

Second, don't become hardened and judgmental. Unfairness and injustice drive many people to bestow upon themselves the responsibility of judging other people's behavior and motives. That self-assignment carries at least two hazards. First, it is God's job to judge, not ours. Second, we rarely have all of the facts connected to any situation. Therefore, we should guard against becoming judgmental in times of unfairness.

Third, don't become resistant and disbelieving. Men who have been burned easily become distrustful of anyone, anytime, for anything. They insert another layer of barrier between them and friends, and even between them and their own healthy attitudes. They live the life of a doubting Thomas, which can become a very negative influence on any work team.

9. *Fail without failing*

A failure is not someone who has tried and failed; it is someone who has given up trying and resigned himself to failure; it is not a condition, but an attitude.
—Sydney J. Harris

When we think of David in the Bible, we obviously think of a very successful king—a man whose life was aligned after God's own heart. But our viewpoint of his career is always from the end looking back. It ended well. He was very successful. However, the word *successful* is not always the word we would attach to every snapshot of his personal and professional life. Some of his life was spent in situations of failure. David was a convicted murderer, adulterer, and fugitive. Yet at the end of his career, God was willing to evaluate his motives and performance by proclaiming, "David was a man after mine own heart."

The cover story of *Fortune* magazine (May 1, 1995) was titled "So You Fail. Now Bounce Back!" It was a story that chronicled the failure and recovery of twenty key American executives. Among the lessons was that debacles and disasters will happen. Such experience is common to all. What is not common is how we weather those storms and quakes and how life turns out.[14]

The difference is clearly the character factor. One could argue, "If a man had such good character in the first place, why did he fail and falter?" That case can be argued. However, the question is not how to minimize our failures, which could have been another study, but rather how to handle failure when it occurs. Character doesn't look for someone to blame. It doesn't try to relabel the failure to something more appealing as the cause. It doesn't throw in the towel of confidence and hope and accept defeat. It squares up its shoulders, like David did in Psalm 51, and admits to full or partial participation. It analyzes enough to extract principles for future improvement. It might try to fix the problem, or it might simply say, "I'm sorry, please forgive me." And then it focuses on the future, not the past, and moves on.

10. *Successfully handle success*

Looks aren't everything.
Luxury is not everything.
Money is not everything.
Health is not everything.
Success is not everything.
Happiness is not everything.
Even everything is not everything.
There's more to life than everything.[15]

"Success means attaining some measure of money, fame, power, and self-fulfillment—and then looking the part."[16] That is the way one man defined it. For certain, our culture sees success as synonymous with achievement and accomplishment. Success tests a man's character more accurately than failure. It lays bare our motivations and puts a body on our theology.

Recently I received a phone call from a friend candidating for a COO position in a $100 million company. He is a battle-trained veteran of business. He told me he was thinking of withdrawing his name from the recruiters' short list. His reason was that the founder/CEO seemed to be drunk on his own success. Sometimes that attitude appears as a self-involved one-way conversation. Sometimes it appears as false humility, constantly saying, "We're not sure why we're successful; we're just doing our best."

So, what is a successful man supposed to think, and how should he act regarding his own success?

1. *Be careful not to ever let success rearrange the order of the universe.* We are not the center of the universe. We are not even a planet. Each of us is one person, residing on one planet. Sometimes success has a way of rearranging all of the components of our universe. That would make for a humorous map to be stretched across the office wall.

2. *Be careful not to ever let success be defined or measured without the God factor.* Ronald Reagan used to tell a story about two fellows who were out hiking in the woods and suddenly looked up and saw a grizzly bear coming over the hill toward them. One of them immediately reached into his pack, pulled out a pair of sneakers, and started removing his boots and putting on the sneakers. The other one standing there said, "You don't think you can outrun that grizzly, do you?" And the first one said, "I don't have to, I just have to

be able to outrun you." For many people, success is only defined and measured in the horizontal. "It is my performance against yours." Certainly that performance comparison can be of some help to guide continuous improvement. But success must have a vertical component also. There is the God factor. A man of character realizes this and religiously blends God's role into all his achievements.

3. *Be careful not to ever think that past success continually means future success.* One of the biggest dangers of success is an arrogance of presumption that can cultivate in the hardened mind of the successful. The story is told of the man who went to his boss's office one Monday morning. His boss gave him a $50 bill and said, "I just want you to know how good of a job you did this last week." The next Monday the same thing happened. The next Monday the same thing, and the next Monday the same thing. On the fifth week, the boss didn't call. The worker was furious, called his wife, and threatened to quit. It is so easy for us to lose a tight grip on the slippery emotion of arrogance and presumption.

Conclusion

I f every Christian man would evidence sterling, sturdy character in the workplace, a chain reaction of evangelism would result. The non-Christians in our work world need the words and actions of Christianity to be melded within one person. We must display good character; then we may begin telling the good news of Jesus Christ. Character matters.

So it was with David the shepherd, the musician, the soldier, and the king. So it is with all of us. A life without character will unravel. To be honest, it might not come apart until after we are gone, like Armand Hammer, but it will be exposed. But the good news is that the same principle applied to David's life. God saw David as a man with a heart of wholeness or integrity who pleased Him across the span of his life. Now there is a hero worth following!

Where Do I Go from Here?

1. *Pray.*

   Don't try to make improvements on your character without God. Carve out a few minutes every day and discuss your "character condition" with the Lord.

2. *Ask.*

   Have three talks soliciting feedback on your character. Ask your spouse, ask your children, and ask a friend to help you honestly gauge your character development.

3. *Identify.*

   Put your finger on two specific facets of your character that could use an overhaul. Write down your goal on a three-by-five-inch card and keep it with you for thirty days. Go ahead and list out some strategies that will help you achieve your goal.

4. *Read.*

   With a pen in hand, read through either Daniel's or Nehemiah's life in the Old Testament looking for examples of positive character development.

5. *Assess.*

   Do a quick assessment of the relationships in your life, and define which are constructive towards positive character development and which are destructive.

6. *Share.*

   Find a circle of friends to share with. Add the sharp edge of accountability to your good intentions.

7. *Give.*

   Make sure you're not trying to grow a clean life from a dirty heart. Give your life to Christ if you've never done that.

Notes

Chapter One

1. Edward J. Epstein, *Dossier: The Secret History of Armand Hammer* (New York: Random House, 1996).

Chapter Two

1. James M. Kouzes and Barry Z. Posner, *Leadership Challenge* (San Fransisco: Jossey-Bass Publishers, 1987), pp. 17-19.

Chapter Three

1. Pat Morley, *Man in the Mirror: Solving the Twenty-Four Problems Men Face* (Nashville: Thomas Nelson Publishers, Inc., 1992), p. 262.
2. Tom Peters, *Thriving on Chaos* (New York: Vintage Books, a Division of Random House, 1987).
3. "Smedes, Larson Highlight Scholars Week," *Southwestern News,* April 1983, p. 7.
4. David Augsburg, *Caring Enough to Forgive* (Ventura, California: Regal Books, 1981), p. 8.

5. Sherwood Wirt and Kersten Beckstrom, *Topical Encyclopedia of Living Quotations* (Minneapolis, Minnesota: Bethany House Publishers, 1982), p. 50.

6. Edyth Draper, *Draper's Book of Quotations for the Christian World* (Wheaton, Illinois: Tyndale House Publishers, Inc., 1992).

7. J. B. Phillips, *Letters to Young Churches* (New York: The Macmillan Company, 1958), p. 108.

8. Stephen Covey, *Principle-Centered Leadership* (New York: Fireside: Simon & Schuster, Inc., 1992), p. 137-8.

9. Peter Senge, *The Fifth Discipline* (New York: Bantam/Doubleday, 1994).

10. Peter F. Drucker, *The Effective Executive* (New York: Perinnial Library, Harper & Row, 1966, 1967), pp. 25-26.

11. Morely, p. 133.

12. Draper.

13. Daniel Taylor, *Cynicism* (Downers Grove, Illinois: InterVarsity, 1982), p. 5.

14. Patricia Sellers, "So You Fail. Now Bounce Back!" *Fortune*, 1 May 1995.

15. Steve Turner and Dennis Haack, *The Rest of Success* (Nashville: Thomas Nelson Publishers, Inc., 1991), p. 50.

16. Ibid., p. 40.

If you liked this book and would like to know more about ᵀᴴᴱLife@Work Co.™ or Cornerstone please call us at 1-800-739-7863.

Other ways to reach us:

Mail: Post Office Box 1928
          Fayetteville, AR 72702

Fax: (501) 443-4125

E-mail: LifeWork@CornerstoneCo.com